Created by Sean LIV & Jason Glynn

Flourish

by

AZURIDGE

ISBN 978-0-9813986-6-2

Flourish
by
AZURIDGE

The Flourish Journal is your foundation to your own path of transformation. Created for Azuridge's Flourish - The LIV Well Spa, the Flourish Journal follows the Azuridge's pillars:

Be Inspired, Be Creative, Be Connected, Be Transformed and Be Here.

Each section invites you to be present, reflect, and set intentions in these areas, with inspiring tips and advice for tapping into supplemental crystal energy.

You can be the foundation for the changes you want to make in your life. We have the ability to make many small changes that lead to something amazing. Flourish - The LIV Well Spa believes in living a life in full colour, grounding and nourishing the seeds to our ultimate potential.

Let the Flourish Journal inspire your journey.

Contents

Dedication

This journal is dedicated to two very special people.
Who believed and inspired us to be
Creative, and Inspired.
Together, we built a place of Transformation.

This book is our way to thank them by providing you a platform to
journal your thoughts -
to Be inspired, to Be Creative and to Be Connected
so that you can be Transformed.

Introduction

Introduction

This journal is designed to inspire you to awaken to the possibility within you. There is a vast amount of potential with in each of us ready to be uncovered. Now more than ever is the time for all of us to stand up in our lives and make it count. Now more than ever do we need to dig deep and make our lives matter - both for us and also for generations to come.

Time is all we have - and it goes by quicker and quicker each day. Learning how to be present and approach each day with awareness is vital. It's time to plant the seeds that will bring our lives into mindfulness and beauty.

At Flourish - The LIV Well Spa, we believe in living a life in full colour. This means the full spectrum of the rainbow - living brightly in all areas by grounding and nourishing the seeds to our ultimate potential.

So now take a deep breath and see what it means for you to Flourish in your life. There are no right or wrong answers here - just a little seed of inspiration for your life to come to you.

To Flourish for me is to...

BE INSPIRED — TO BE INSPIRED IS THE FULL SPECTRUM OF COLOUR RADIATING LIGHT WITHIN YOU

BE CONNECTED — TO BE CONNECTED IS LIVING YOUR LIFE THROUGH YOUR HEART, LET GO AND LET YOUR HEART LEAD THE WAY

BE CREATIVE — TO BE CREATIVE IS TO ALLOW THE UNIVERSAL ENERGY TO EXPRESS ITSELF THROUGH YOU

BE TRANSFORMED — TO BE TRANSFORMED IS TRANSCENDING THE OLD BELIEFS TO LIVE AS THE UNSTOPPABLE HUMAN YOU WERE BORN TO BE

BE HERE — TO BE HERE IS TO LIVE IN THE MOMENT - BE PRESENT, FEEL AND EXPERIENCE LIFE THROUGH THE GIFTS OF YOUR SENSES.

Through the following pages you will notice that the journal is broken up in five main areas.

BE INSPIRED BE CONNECTED BE CREATIVE BE TRANSFORMED BE HERE

In each area, take note on how you are using your energy. As the old saying goes, energy flows where the attention goes. We all deserve to live a life of happiness, joy and prosperity. Yes we all have our challenges, but maybe they are the substance we add to our seeds to reach our ultimate potential.

We would love to hear what it means for you to Flourish, so please send us your meaning and email it to flourish@azuridgehotel.com.

Each spring we write all meanings on seeded paper and plant them in our Flourish garden outside in our nature space.

Please don't be shy, lets all grow together

LIV a Life in Full Colour

To create a life you want to live, you must first become present. Pause and reflect on where you have been, and what choices you are making. What values do you have? What do you stand for? Once you become present, allow yourself to be transformed by the energy in the following pages. As you do, you might notice what beliefs are merely unconsciously-stored belief patterns that have been passed down to you. Whether good or bad, it just is - unleash you and show up as the being you are!

Our Five Pillars

The five pillars here at Azuridge are the fundamental aspects of life. Each BE is part of who we are as a company, but it is also our way of life. We want to share them as part of the legacy we hope you will build for yourself.

How to Use This Journal

This journal is a simple way to plant seeds and watch them grow. Each section features inspirational ideas, a crystal related to each of our five pillars, as well as pages for you to journal in. Whether you keep this journal in your nightstand, on your desk, or in your closet, realize that whatever you do, we are here supporting you to flourish in your own way.

The Reason

We are here on this planet living our lives in this time and space, and if we are the creators of our lives and destiny then we can create something magical. Can you imagine if we all showed up not only for ourselves, but we were the change we wished to see? What an elevated world would that be!
Ponder that for a minute!

Pillar

BE INSPIRED

1

Liv Inspired

To be inspired is contagious - everyone around you feels that energy! It's that feeling you get when you know you are on the right path. It's the amazement at the possibility laid out before you. It's the fuel that keeps things going. What can you do in your life to create the feeling of being INSPIRED?

Amethyst

THE STONE OF INNER STRENGTH & PURIFYING

Amethyst

THE STONE OF INNER STRENGTH & PURIFYING

Clarity, Wisdom, Inner Eye, Opening of high self, Perception

Crystal Properties:

The amethyst is associated with the third eye and crown chakras, which represent intuition and our connection to the universe, respectively. It's useful in meditation, bringing peace, relaxation, and a greater spiritual connection. This lovely purple crystal is one of the most powerful and popular ones in the world.

Crystal Knowledge:

Did you know crystals give off a vibration that can change your own energy field? They can set the tone in your living space as well. A crystal's energy can be felt and not seen. Why not create an inspiring living space by adding a few crystals to the decor in your home, office or bedroom? Your energy field will thank you!

Be Inspired

1) Listen to a different style of music
2) Learn to meditate
3) Learn to dance
4) Read an autobiography
5) Take a break from social media
6) Take a break from the news
7) Breathe deep!
8) Learn about the anatomy of our body
9) Learn about our solar system
10) Learn the history of your family
11) Learn to cook
12) Do something that scares you
13) Find a life song and listen to it often
14) Reconnect with an old friend
15) Share stories with a loved one
16) Get back into nature
17) Read a book with a child
18) Organize your home
19) Enjoy some gentle yoga
20) Daydream

Use the following pages for journaling, or create your own Be Inspired list.

No. 1

 Pillar 1

No. 2

No. 3

No. 4

No. 5

Pillar 1

No. 6

No. 7

Pillar 1

No. 8

No. 9

No. 10

No. 11

No. 12

No. 13

No. 14

No. 15

No. 16

No. 17

Pillar 1

No. 18

No. 19

No. 20

Pillar

BE CONNECTED

2

Liv Connected

We are all connected. What we do in our own lives affects the collective as well. We first need to connect with ourselves. We need to be grounded in our own essence to be able to plug into the world around us. Then, we can see the mystery of life, nature and our universe. Most of all, if we are all connected through our heart centre we can then raise the vibration of our planet as a whole.

Rose Quart

THE STONE OF UNCONDITIONAL LOVE & HAR

Rose Quartz

THE STONE OF UNCONDITIONAL LOVE & HARMONY

Trust, Harmony, Self love, Friendship, Oneness

Crystal Properties:

Linked to the heart chakra, rose quartz is all about unconditional love and harmony in relationships. Look to the rose quartz to help you forgive yourself, and encourage feelings of acceptance and trust. Meditating with this crystal will awaken feelings of self-love and oneness.

Crystal Knowledge:

Crystals come from the earth, and it's important to maintain that connection as often as you can. The full moon provides the perfect energy for cleansing crystals - simply leave them out overnight, directly on the earth if possible. Running water, such as a stream, neutralizes negative energy buildup. When cleansing crystals, take this moment to ground yourself in the nature that surrounds you, and give thanks. Take note - direct sunlight can cause some crystals to fade, so be sure to do your research.

Be Connected

1) Hug your loved ones for a minimum of 30 seconds
2) Stand under a a waterfall
3) Teach your dog a new trick
4) Dance like no one is watching
5) Start a book club
6) Volunteer in your community
7) Buy local
8) Share your favourite local business with your circle Place
9) Call a friend or write a letter
10) Say hello and smile at a person you meet
11) At the grocery store or bank, use a clerk and thank them by name
12) Buy a coffee for the person behind you
13) Listen with your heart to someone who needs an ear
14) Leave a gift card in your mailbox for the mail carrier
15) Keep your comments to yourself unless asked for your option
16) Ask your neighbour to borrow some eggs instead of going to the store
17) Give your neighbour something in return
18) Let someone cut in front of you in rush hour traffic peacefully
19) Practice activating your pelvic floor muscles
20) Visualize your ideal version of yourself and live it

Use the following pages for journaling, or create your own Be Connected list

Pillar 2

No. 1

No. 2

No. 3

No. 4

No. 5

Pillar 2

No. 6

No. 7

Pillar 2

No. 8

No. 9

No. 10

No. 11

Pillar 2

No. 12

No. 13

No. 14

No. 15

Pillar 2

No. 16

No. 17

No. 18

No. 19

No. 20

Pillar

BE CREATIVE

3

BE
CREATIVE

TO BE CREATIVE IS TO ALLOW THE
UNIVERSAL ENERGY TO EXPRESS
ITSELF THROUGH YOU

LIV Creatively

Creativity is one of the magic pieces of life. We can all create almost anything! It doesn't have to be a doodle, a painting, or a book. Creativity is when, piece by piece, something great comes together without us really knowing how. We are all creators in our own lives, but it's up to you how and when you tap into your own creative energy. You may not see yourself as a creative person, but trust us - you are! Get into your heart and see these creative juices flow.

Citrine

THE STONE OF SUCCESS, PROSPERITY & PERSONAL POWER

Citrine

THE STONE OF SUCCESS, PROSPERITY & PERSONAL POWER

Success, Prosperity, Power, Self-expression, Optimism

Crystal Properties:
Citrine has a vivid yellow energy, related to its properties of positivity and optimism. Connected to the solar plexus chakra, citrine can enhance self-esteem and encourage powerful transformation. Turn to citrine when you want to reflect on abundance and joy.

Crystal Knowledge:
Did you know crystals give off a vibration that can change your own energy field? They can set the tone in your living space as well. A crystal's energy can be felt and not seen. Why not create an inspiring living space by adding a few crystals to the decor in your home, office or bedroom? Your energy field will thank you!

20 Ways to
Be Creative

1) Live in the present
2) Give your home a facelift
3) Revamp your master bedroom
4) Paint a picture
5) Lean to sew, knit, or crochet
6) Colour coordinate your monthly filing system
7) Doodle   whatever comes to mind!
8) Reorganize your furniture
9) Read an old favourite book
10) Discover a new favourite book
11) Have a movie night and imagine an alternate ending
12) Collect items in nature
13) Create a vision board with images representing a life
    dream
14) Take an art class with a friend
15) Write poetry
16) Look for shapes in clouds
17) Choose a colour to represent your year
18) Choose a word to represent your dreams
19) Write down three major goals for the year ahead
20) First thing in the morning, write down the previous night's
    dream

Use the following pages for journaling, or create your own Be Creative list.

 Pillar 3

No. 1

No. 2

No. 3

No. 4

No. 5

No. 6

No. 7

Pillar 3

No. 8

No. 9

No. 10

No. 11

No. 12

No. 13

Pillar 3

No. 14

No. 15

Pillar 3

No. 16

No. 17

No. 18

No. 19

No. 20

Pillar

BE TRANSFORMED

4

BE

TRANSFORMED

TO BE TRANSFORMED IS TRANSCENDING
THE OLD BELIEFS TO LIVE AS THE
UNSTOPPABLE HUMAN YOU WERE BORN
TO BE.

LIV Transformed

Being transformed means we've given ourselves permission to let go of what's no longer serving us, and using this as the platform for growth. We all have cycles or life lessons we need to go through. Maybe it's a loss of a loved one, a breakdown in a relationship, or even a midlife crisis. But in times like these, we can begin to live again. Life cracks us open for a reason and it's when we are cracked open that the light can seen. If you're going through a transition, don't give up - you have within everything you need to make it through.

Malachite
THE STONE OF TRANSFORMATION

Malachite

THE STONE OF TRANSFORMATION

Transformation, Balance, Intention, Manifesting

Crystal Properties:

Connected to the heart and throat chakras, malachite is a powerful crystal of spiritual transformation and personal growth. It promotes emotional clarity and balance, absorbing negative energies that may be keeping you stuck in the same routines. Malachite helps you move forward with intention.

Crystal Knowledge:

Most crystals will help for only a certain timeframe, until you are ready to move onto the next step on your journey. Keep small piece in your pockets and when the time is right you may feel that you want to give it to someone else who needs it. This not only respects the energy of your crystal, but it means your energy is there to support another person as well. As they old saying goes - Share the LOVE!

20 Ways to

Be Transformed

1) Start an exercise regimen
2) Write a releasement letter and burn it
3) Make peace with the past - the present is now
4) Record that song
5) Write that book you have been pondering for years
6) Sign up for a yoga retreat
7) Take a trip
8) Know your truth and live it
9) Cut your hair off and get a new hairdo
10) Cut ties with toxic relationships
11) Practice setting boundaries
12) Take ownership of yourself
13) Praise your value and own it
14) Don't stop trying
15) Believe in yourself
16) Stop listening to the inner critic
17) Don't judge - be neutral, as we are all on our own paths
18) Stop rushing
19) Stop procrastinating - and get doing!
20) See your glass as half full

Use the following pages for journaling, or create your own Be Transformed list.

Pillar 4

No. 1

No. 2

No. 3

No. 4

No. 5

No. 6

No. 7

No. 8

No. 9

Pillar 4

No. 10

No. 11

No. 12

No. 13

Pillar 4

No. 14

No. 15

No. 16

No. 17

No. 18

No. 19

Pillar 4

No. 20

Pillar
BE HERE

5

BE
HERE

LIV Here

To be here means to live in the moment. Be present, feel and experience life through the gifts of our senses. Learning how to ground yourself in the essence of who you can truly become is a powerful gift. No one is stopping you from living from that place. Look up and see the vast amount of blue sky that surrounds us, and dream big with the beautiful essence of who you can be.

Green Fluorite

THE STONE OF CONNECTION & HEALING

Green Fluorite

THE STONE OF CONNECTION & HEALING

Compassion, Strength, Vitality, Happiness

Crystal Properties:

Green fluorite resonates with the heart chakra, associated with unconditional love, compassion, and personal truth. Green fluorite can encourage focus, intuition. It can also enhance your own personal renewal and insight, enabling you to heal from past hurts and grow.

Crystal Knowledge:

Taking care of the frequency of your crystals is just as important as watering your plants, plugging in your cell phone, or your daily exercise regimen. You should always clear your gems and have an intention for each piece. It's super easy. First, to clear your gems you can place them in the full moonlight, leave them in a river, and then charge them in the sun light. Once charged, let them do their magic for you. They love to be on display, so keep them where they can be seen.

20 Ways to

Be Here

1) Cook your favourite meal
2) Take a long bubble bath
3) Listen to music that matches your mood
4) Cuddle your pet
5) Take some photos of whatever you like
6) Go for a walk, look up and notice what you don't normally see
7) Burn incense or a scented candle
8) Wrap yourself in a blanket and breathe
9) Bake and allow yourself to get messy
10) Ask a loved one about their favourite memories
11) Draw or colour with your child
12) Find a quiet spot in nature and just listen
13) Stand up and stretch slowly
14) Focus on enjoying the colours and flavours of your food
15) Put your phone away during meals
16) Meditate
17) Go for a hike and collect leaves, twigs, and pinecones
18) Take five deep breaths before getting out of bed in the morning
19) Let yourself laugh
20) Park farther away in a parking lot and enjoy the extra few steps

Use the following pages for journaling, or create your own Be Here list.

Pillar 5

No. 1

Pillar 5

No. 2

No. 3

No. 4

No. 5

No. 6

No. 7

No. 8

No. 9

No. 10

No. 11

Pillar 5

No. 12

No. 13

No. 14

No. 15

No. 16

No. 17

No. 18

No. 19

No. 20

To flourish

Is to

In Full

Colour

The inspiration behind the journal

Jason Glynn General Manger & CFO

AZURIDGE

Jason Glynn is the General Manager and CFO of Azuridge. With a background in finance and a long career in the hospitality industry, Jason brings a unique mix of practicality and innovation to Azuridge. Under his guidance, Azuridge has become a retreat like no other, where people and corporations can come together to be inspired, to be together, and to celebrate. Jason is a firm believer in Azuridge's core pillars: Be Inspired, Be Connected, Be Creative, Be Transformed & Be Here.

A proud husband and father of two, Jason is blessed to work with so many amazing people at Azuridge, and is dedicated to helping its guests develop and evolve in all aspects of their lives.

Sean LIV Director of Flourish - The LIV Well Spa

Sean Liv is the visionary program curator, coach, mentor, and teacher of Azuridge's Flourish - The LIV Well Spa. With her signature upbeat personality, energetic outlook, compassionate ear, and expertise in a multitude of health, wellness and spiritual techniques, she uplifts and inspires people every day.

After deciding to overhaul all areas of her life and set a new path, Sean built her career as a Transformational Coach, inspiring speaker, author of The Ticket, and founder of The Ticket to Change, a transformational program for the mind, body, and spirit. She is also the host of the Liv Daily Show, an upbeat health and wellness show airing on CTV. She's passionate about helping people find the deep motivation that makes them unstoppable in connecting with their dreams.

Sean Liv encourages others to build a lifestyle that focuses on positive body, mind, and spiritual routines. Her own transformation journey gave her the tools to help people find life, inspiration and vitality.

Our Property

AZURIDGE

BE INSPIRED **BE** CONNECTED **BE** CREATIVE **BE** TRANSFORMED

Come and experience a private world of luxury like no other. The Azuridge is nestled in the beautiful rolling Alberta foothills, 20 minutes from Calgary. Enjoy a personalized luxury hotel experience whether you are staying overnight, enjoying fine dining at the Opal restaurant, here for a corporate meeting or joining us for one of our exclusive gatherings, we are at your service so you can just simply be here.

FLOURISH

THE LIV WELL SPA AT AZURIDGE

At Flourish – The LIV Well Spa at Azuridge, we take self care to a higher level.

Flourish is a transformative wellness centre, blending the healing powers of crystal energy, essential oils, and chakra flow with traditional spa experiences. Flourish is a calming space for workshops, exercise classes, yoga, meditation, personal reflection, and self-improvement. Our focus is the powerful balance of mind, body, and spirit. We are proud to offer these inspiring services online to members.

The Flourish journal is a perfect complement to our online membership program, empowering you to move higher in your journey.

For more information,
download our app on your Samsung, Apple or Android device
or visit us at azuridgehotel.com/wellness

A special
Thank you

AZURIDGE

Thank you

We would like to thank all of the staff at AZURIDGE for their INSPIRATION, CREATIVITY and CONNECTION to AZURIDGE.

It is together that we were able to create a transformational experience to all of our guests.

&

To Samantha, thank you for making our words transform into magic.

CPSIA information can be obtained
at www.ICGtesting.com
Printed in the USA
BVHW012024271220
596501BV00010B/178